Traffic

Traffic

New and Selected Prose Poems

Jack Anderson

THE

MARIE

ALEXANDER

POETRY

SERIES

New Rivers Press
1998

First Edition
Manufactured in the United States of America for New Rivers Press
Library of Congress Catalog Card Number: 98-66584
ISBN: 0-89823-191-4
Edited by C.W. Truesdale
Copyedited by Joanne Fish
Book design and typesetting by Percolator
Marie Alexander Poetry Series, No. 1

New Rivers Press is a nonprofit literary press dedicated to publishing the very best emerging writers in our region, nation, and world.

The publication of *Traffic* has been made possible by support from Robert Alexander; the Bush Foundation; the Minnesota State Arts Board (through an appropriation by the Minnesota Legislature and the National Endowment for the Arts); the Beim Foundation; the McKnight Foundation; the Star Tribune Foundation; and the contributing members of New Rivers Press.

MINNESOTA
STATE ARTS BOARD

NATIONAL
ENDOWMENT
FOR THE
ARTS

New Rivers Press
420 North 5th Street, Suite 910
Minneapolis, MN 55401

www.mtn.org/newrivpr

Acknowledgments

Some of these works first appeared in the following publications: "The Model Community" was originally published in *Caliban.* "Traffic" was originally published in *Caprice.* "The Mysterious Barricades; or, The Enchaînments of Memory" was originally published in *Chelsea.* "The Adventures of Bucky Badger" was originally published in *Exquisite Corpse.* "Your Last Phone Call" was originally published in *5 AM.* "The Pregnant Teapot" was originally published in *Giants Play Well in the Drizzle.* "Golden Moment" and "Research Topics" were originally published in *Hanging Loose.* "He Lives Among Us" was originally published in *Poetry East.* "The Somnambulists' Hotel," "Moral Discourse," "My Mother Growing Old," "Angels," and "A Window in the Poem" were originally published in *The Prose-Poem: An International Journal.* "The Sincere Poet" was originally published in *Transfer.*

Other works appeared in my previous books: "Snow" was originally published in *The Hurricane Lamp* (NEW Books/The Crossing Press, 1969). "The White Chapter" from *The Invention of New Jersey,* by Jack Anderson, © 1969. Reprinted by permission of the University of Pittsburgh Press. "Thimbleism," "Orpheus in the Afternoon," "Phalaris and the Bull: A Story and an Examination," "A Reading of This Poem," and "The Party Train" were originally published in *City Joys* (Release Press, 1975). "Connections," "Calamitous Dreams," "Bartenders," "Sunday Dinner," "Return to Work," "True or False Quiz," and "Abandoned Cities" from *Toward the Liberation of the Left Hand,* by Jack Anderson, © 1977. Reprinted by permission of the University of Pittsburgh Press. "The Burden," "Once Each Spring the Face of Ophelia Appears Upon the Waters," and "His Story" were originally published in *The Dust Dancers* (Bk/Mk Press, 1977). "The Mysterious Sound" was originally published in *The Clouds of That Country* (Hanging Loose Press, 1982). "A Poem of Coffee," "A Journey by Railroad," and "Life on the Moon" were originally published in *Field Trips on the Rapid Transit* (Hanging Loose Press, 1990).

Contents

III. Journeys

To George

I.
Wonders

Connections

———

We are all connected, one unto another.

A bulb in my hallway has burned out. I keep fitting new bulbs into the socket. Nothing happens.

Then I find in my hallway a switch I have never noticed before. I flick it on and off, on and off. Nothing happens.

Three blocks away, in their apartment, a wife calls to her husband, "Henry! Come quick! The lights seem to be going on and off for no reason."

Thimbleism

I was riding the Staten Island ferry one evening when I noticed a woman on deck wiggling her fingers at the sky. When she wiggled the fingers of her left hand, the stars twinkled in the left half of the sky. When she wiggled the fingers of her right hand, the stars twinkled in the right half of the sky. When she wiggled the fingers of both hands, all the stars twinkled together.

I stared at her for a long time. At last I could not help but ask, "How do you do that, ma'am?"

"It's easy," she said. "Just wiggle your left fingers like this. Just wiggle your right fingers like that."

I tried it. She was right: it was easy. Soon the stars were twinkling in the sky whenever I wiggled my fingers.

Fascinated by my new powers, I kept wiggling my fingers harder and harder. The harder I wiggled, the brighter the stars twinkled. After one great flurry of ten fingers in unison, the heavens opened with a thunderclap and there in a blaze of light was the pyramid on the back of the dollar bill—except that at the top of the pyramid was not an open eye, but a gold thimble. Suddenly, my right hand was trying to push a pen like a needle across a piece of paper, and the thimble descended from the sky to help me. "This is your gift," cried a voice from a cloud.

"Thank you," I shouted back, and after writing this down I took off the thimble and put it in my pocket.

When I reached home and told my neighbor what had happened, he said, "It's too bad you don't live in the backwoods South. Because there you could gather all the superstitious people in the county and set yourself up as the leader of a new sect dedicated to the worship of the holy thimble. You could call your faith Thimbleism. You'd make a mint off those hicks. But here in New York no one will believe you. You'll never get famous and you'll never get rich."

A Poem of Coffee

Sometimes, even as you drink it, you cannot say how it tastes. Yet you keep on drinking it, day and night.

It is the winter morning with the snow still falling. The summer morning with the light on the curtains. It is the hot summer night in the greasy spoon, the cold winter night there because the car won't start, when you sit for hours with nothing to do. It is the lead in pencils, the ink in pens. It is riding the el past kitchen windows. It is a porch light left on. A light left on at the back of the house.

It is a snowy morning in winter, a summer light on the curtains. It is the drive across Ohio. The drive across Texas. Trucks shifting gears. The way a Greyhound bus smells. It is listening to the men with murmuring voices who play records on FM all through the night. It is driving at night with the car radio booming. It is long talks with Mother. Chain-smoking cigarettes. And an ashtray filled with cigarette stubs. A press room. A seminar room. A county jail in the sticks. It is waiting to change buses. Waiting to change trains in dim, empty stations. It is staying up late. Or getting up early. It is the first thing after toothpaste. The last thing before bed.

It is the winter morning with the snow still falling, the summer morning with the light on the curtains. It is a habit, a ritual. Your job. Your small pleasure. It is what keeps you going day after day, what makes you get by on your nerves alone. It is what you take in with the Sunday paper. It is printing, a black typeface. And a piece of white paper without any words. It is darkness in the pencil, snow on the page.

It is this piece of white paper with this snow still falling, this light on the curtains, this pencil writing. It is these words before you, any time of the year, any time, any day.

The Mysterious Sound

———

In one scene of Chekhov's *The Cherry Orchard* the characters, while on an excursion to the countryside, hear amidst the stillness of the fields a mysterious sound they cannot identify. Various tentative explanations for it are proffered, each in its own way faintly ridiculous. This scene embarrasses, yet fascinates, actors. It is unlike any other scene they are ever called upon to play. It makes them feel they are no longer in control of things. And yet they are obsessed by that sound and by its place in that scene.

Such sounds do exist. And they are not ridiculous. They are not ridiculous simply because they resist our explanations completely. Such sounds are everywhere.

If, instead of being out in the country, those characters in Chekhov had been in a great city—the same city in which the actors probably are—and had they listened closely there, those characters and those actors might have heard other sounds equally mysterious. These:

There is the sound you hear while sitting in your apartment when the streets grow still and there comes this low sigh, this low sigh slowly repeated at regular intervals, this sigh that is almost a musical note, a repeated note like a bell, like a tolling bell sighing. It seems to come out of the bricks of buildings, out of all the buildings together, a universal mineral exhalation which is gone now because a truck has run over it. But you have heard it,

just as, at night by the docks, you have heard the groan of wood, the feeble wood of old piers trying to reach across the water, unable to reach all the way across. Yet across the water comes an answer: a hum like the hum of someone singing to herself as she packs her bags to join someone distant, a hum like the hum of electric wires bearing messages to a place even farther in the distance. Soon it's no longer quite there. No longer there at all. Then you wonder whether you even heard it,

just as you wonder what those sounds were that you heard when, as a child, you woke up in the middle of the night: the sound in the garden (which might have been rain), the sound down cellar (which might have been the furnace), the sound that sounded like someone going up and down stairs (which might have been your parents or your sisters going up and down the real stairs). Except these were not merely the sounds of rain, of a furnace, or of people on stairs—they were the sounds you heard when waking up in the middle of the night you were a child. And as they grew fainter and went away, you fell asleep. Then when they were gone away you were fast asleep, and when you woke up you were older, and when you were older still they were all gone and you couldn't quite account for them,

just as you can't quite account for the sound you first identify as a train pulling out, leaving the city. But then you remember that this city has no railroad tracks, so how could there be trains? And then you remember that this city has buried its railroad tracks, and you think you hear trains deep beneath the streets, the sound of departing trains rising out of gratings, sewers, and manhole covers, out of ventilation shafts and cracks in the pavement. However you hear it, that train is leaving. Whatever its sound is, that sound is fading.

But what you name that sound—the tolling bell sound, the pier at night sound, the sound of childhood, the train sound—is not necessarily what that sound is. It is only the role you have assigned to that sound. Furthermore,

all such sounds are forever fading. They never come nearer. They never come close to you. They are always receding,

they have nothing to do with you no matter how much you try to name them, you cannot get close to them. They are going away from you. Going away.

Calamitous Dreams

———

He dreamed the old woman he had jeered at in the street took off all his clothes and wrapped him in a squirrelskin. Then he was set among the other squirrels and guinea pigs who were very well mannered and waited on the old woman. First he learned to clean her walnut-shell shoes. Then he learned to catch little moths and grind them into flour, from which he baked a soft white bread. When he awoke, he discovered his nose had grown down to his chin, his hands were covered with warts, and though his belly was round as a barrel, he tottered about on matchstick legs. He was even uglier than the old woman herself. The squirrels and guinea pigs ran chittering after him.

*

He was dreaming about the cat he let starve. He dreamed his cat left town and lived beside the road. If anyone passed, it devoured him. If a cow went past, the cat devoured it. If a goat went past, the cat devoured it. Whoever went along the road, the cat devoured. When he awoke, he found himself in the cat's belly. He had been devoured by the cat while he slept. Then he was digested. And that was the end of him.

*

Ever since he could remember, there was a sword growing out of him. When he was a little boy, it was a little sword. As he grew older and bigger, the sword grew bigger, too. Now that he was grown up, it was very big. One night, he had a dream. He dreamed the sword was really a penis. But when he awoke, he discovered it was only a sword after all.

*

He dreamed his country had been changed. Earth and water, trees and plants, birds and beasts, all looked the same as before, but what struck terror into his heart was the silence that reigned. Not a rustle could be heard. Birds sat on their branches with heads erect and swelling throats, but his ear caught nothing. Dogs opened their mouths as if to

———

bark, the toiling oxen seemed about to bellow, but neither bark nor bellow reached him. When he came to the city, people were running through the streets, yet he heard no footfall, and other people stood at their windows, their mouths open as though screaming, yet there was no sound. When he awoke, the people were still at their windows and there was no sound for a long time. Then a voice in the street rang out, "This is what became of us while you slept on." And when he tried to answer, he felt his voice die in his throat.

The Burden

———

There is a kind of joy found only at the end of waiting, the joy of a man who, after days of anxiety, of bruising himself against his own thoughts, masters his embarrassment and registers at a clinic for venereal diseases. Many are before him and have been there for hours. As each newcomer enters, they gaze at him, appraise his case, place silent bets on his probable condition, and smile very faintly among themselves. It is a smile of men who share a secret, a fraternal smile. He, too, learns to smile that smile, for he must take his place in line and the examinations are slow. He waits in a chair. He hardly moves. He holds a magazine, but does not read it. In the distance he hears the rattle of instruments behind the closed doors of surgeries. Little else happens. The helplessness of waiting at last becomes in itself a calm, like sleep. Finally, it is his turn. Almost as though he had resigned his body in ages past and were standing far off, detached from it, watching, he allows the doctor to examine him and make tests, repeated tests, tests whose results are not known quickly. And so he must wait again in line, now in this hallway, now in that laboratory, or outside some other consulting room. Shame no longer matters. Fear, too, has been left behind. All that remains is endurance and, beyond endurance—the reward of endurance—a faint murmur of healing. He hears the doctor murmur, "Now then. Very well. Well now, let's see. Yes. Yes. Yes, indeed. Well then, that will be all. Yes, that will be all now. Nothing to worry about. I assure you, you are fine." Then he reenters the street, emptied of every feeling except the feeling of knowing that he is alive. And it floods him and, for a long time, until the next time, it is more than enough, more than enough.

———

The Somnambulists' Hotel

———

Only sleepwalkers stay there. When they get to town, something draws them to the place, even if they already have reservations somewhere else. Checking in, smiling shyly, they glance about the lobby. Yet they give no sign they are in any way special. And, like everyone else, they see the sights or do business by day and spend their evenings in restaurants or theatres.

But late at night all return to their rooms at the very same time and almost in unison switch off their lights and climb into bed. Their hearts beat faster in happy expectation, yet they cannot say why. Soon, sleep comes to them all.

Then in each room, as the moonlight pours in, a sudden wind lifts the sheets off the beds and sets them swirling. The guests rise up too. Still deep in sleep, they step out of bed while the sheets drop behind them like swaddling bands or shrouds.

Some leap to the window ledges and teeter above the street. Others climb the fire escape to the roof where they race back and forth, holding their heads high and throwing their arms wide in the glimmering starlight.

Some—after opening their closets and finding strange apparel there—put on these garments and venture into the corridors. Clinging to the walls, some struggle in the wind that has now become a great gale. Yet in another corridor only a gentle breeze blows. Women in white nightgowns float through these halls, skimming along in toe shoes, lighted candles in their hands, their long hair streaming loose behind them.

Other guests take the elevator down to the lobby. Fluttering aigrette

———

fans, women in century-old evening dress glide past the night clerk (who never looks up from his paperback novel) and waltz around the ballroom to music only they can hear. Whirling deliriously and breathing harder, they pelt each other with lilies, then stagger as if ready to fall in a swoon.

Yet when City Hall clock strikes the first hour of dawning and the garbagemen come banging along, the guests quiet down and, after fumbling their way back to their rooms, lock the doors, and sink into bed.

You can find them the next morning at breakfast in the coffee shop. They are quiet, all of them, and very reserved. Each sits alone. No one speaks. Yet each looks rested and curiously content.

All at that moment are trying to remember something that happened to them in the night, something their minds cannot quite piece together, but something they know was strangely nice, they decide. They smile their shy smiles and glance about at all the nice people. Surely there must be some secret they share. Buttered toast is chewed in meditation. And all vow to stay here should fate ever lead them this way again.

Once Each Spring the Face of Ophelia Appears Upon the Waters

———

She drifts with the current on her back. No one sees her. Not the clouds above. Nor the gardeners on the bank. The huge barge floating toward her does not see her. Nor does the bargeman sweating in the sun. They will pass over her. As will the pleasure boat with its turning wheel. When the river calms again, the imprint of her face will still be on the water. The clouds will roll downstream like drawings of organ music.

———

Orpheus in the Afternoon

All afternoon, the head of Orpheus rests on a polished tabletop. His hair is cut like that of a student from the School of Fine Arts. His eyes are closed. At sunset the tabletop turns to deep water. The head of Orpheus starts to sink. His eyes open. He sings and is gone. Someone's lover sets a wine bottle and two glasses on the table. The wine in the bottle is dark. The song remains on the phonograph, darker than wine. The daylight fades. It is time for us to eat dinner, it is time to drink wine. To turn on a light would be wrong.

The Mysterious Barricades; or, The Enchaînments of Memory

—

(A Free Fantasia on Themes from the Ballet)
To the Ghost of Joseph Cornell

Surely you have heard this great keyboard piece by Couperin, played either on the harpsichord or on a modern piano. It is a haunting composition.

But what does its title mean—"The Mysterious Barricades"? There have been scores of hypothetical explanations, including some abstruse ones which speculate that certain of the work's distinctive harmonic progressions form sonic blocks or barricades between one phrase and the next. Perhaps this may be true.

However, other theories exist. One wildly romantic—yet given its origin, decidedly intriguing—story about the title was related to me years ago by my first ballet teacher, Michel Enikoff, when I was still a child in Milwaukee.

What an odd little man he was. I have no idea what his age may have been. But, as he reminded us often, he had been trained at the Imperial Russian Ballet School in St. Petersburg and had toured with the Diaghilev Ballets Russes in its earliest seasons.

He had never been a star. Enikoff loved to reminisce, yet refused to puff himself up. He had been in the *corps de ballet*—that was all. However, he said, as a member of the ensemble he had danced in the *corps* of such legendary Diaghilev productions as *Prince Igor,* *Petrouchka,* and *Les Sylphides.* And from time to time, he told us, he was awarded tiny solo parts: he was one of Marc Antony's lieutenants in *Cléopâtre;* in *Carnaval,* he dashed across the stage as the mysterious reveler in the devil's mask, and he was once cast as the mischievous cabin boy in the Sinbad the Sailor episode of *Schéhérazade.*

How he had found his way to Milwaukee was never clear. Yet he had taught there for years, and had his own little following.

One day, Enikoff unexpectedly gathered his children's class around him and regaled us with a strange story. He declared in advance that we would find it incredible. Nevertheless, he said, it had been passed down from one generation of dancers, teachers, and students at the Imperial School to the next. Perhaps the tale came to be embellished a bit over the years. Perhaps each person who told it remembered a few details differently, just as the stager of a classic ballet sometimes knows variations unfamiliar to other *régisseurs*. However, he recalled, everyone in St. Petersburg insisted that the account was basically accurate. And it had much to do with "The Mysterious Barricades."

As everyone knows, he said, the Imperial Court of St. Petersburg was perpetually and passionately Francophile in its taste. Therefore it was inevitable that, one year, an invitation went out to Marie Taglioni, the ballerina who had become the toast of Paris. Even though traveling through Russia would not be easy, she agreed to perform there—for how could she refuse so illustrious an offer?

She took with her a group of musicians familiar with her preferences in tempo and rubato and a small female *corps de ballet,* for the canny *étoile* rightly suspected that the Petersburg noblemen would be smitten by Parisian charmers.

The *corps de ballet* and musicians went ahead in coaches. But Taglioni had a luxuriously appointed carriage all to herself. Although it was midwinter and the snow was deep, the journey proved uneventful until, suddenly one morning in the midst of a Russian nowhere, the carriage came to an abrupt halt. Excited voices could be heard arguing. But gunshots soon silenced the dispute. Someone threw open the door of Taglioni's carriage and she found herself confronted by a scowling man with a bristly black beard and burning eyes. "Dance!" he ordered. "Dance, esteemed ballerina. Dance for me!"

She stepped in amazement out of her carriage. The threatening man was a bandit chief, and he was accompanied by members of his gang—every one of them a cutthroat. Yet what did they want of Taglioni? Her gold? Her celebrated diamond necklace that she always carried with her? No. Not at all. The ballerina's fame had reached them and they desired nothing more than to see her perform.

To that end, they had attacked the coaches with the musicians and the dancers and had forced the women of the *corps de ballet* to line up as a set of human barricades blocking the road, so that if Taglioni had tried to escape in her carriage she would have had to knock down and run over her own dancers. There they stood now, posed *en pointe* like the Wilis in *Giselle*, Taglioni's own favorite ballet and greatest triumph. "Dance!" the bandit growled again. "Dance, my treasured ballerina! Dance!"

And she did, to the accompaniment of her flutists and fiddlers. Taglioni found to her amazement that the snow had frozen so hard and that she was so light that she could skim *sur les pointes* across the tops of the snowbanks while her *corps de ballet* continued to serve as the road's picturesque barricades. When she had finished her *pas seul,* the bandit nearly crushed her with enthusiastic bear hugs and, instead of seizing her possessions, he opened his own strongboxes and loaded her down with all the jewels he had stolen in recent weeks. Then, after embracing her one more time, he let the ballerina and her entourage proceed toward St. Petersburg.

Now it so happened that among the musicians traveling with Taglioni was none other than Couperin. And when he got home to Paris he composed a musical memento of that remarkable adventure: "The Mysterious Barricades."

We sat there enthralled as Enikoff finished his account. "Extraordinary, isn't it?" he said at last. "Yet this is the story they told me at the Imperial School, and why would they tell it if it were not true?"

A long pause followed. None of us wished to move. Then our teacher clapped his hands. "Now, dear children," he said, "We've had enough of this. It is time for class. Ballet is a strict, rational, scientific system. It may deal with fantasies, yet it has no place for fancy. Fancy is unstable. But ballet is exact, unambiguous. Everything about it is clear and hard—as hard as the snow on which Taglioni danced. So take your places at the *barre!* The lesson begins."

His Story

He had gone to visit a once-famous pianist, now blind and living in retirement in a country house far from anywhere. A faithful old servant showed him inside. But he became annoyed because the servant refused to take him to his master immediately. He became so resentful that he struck the servant with a cane he found propped against a chair. The servant fell unconscious to the floor just as the pianist entered the room. The pianist was not angry because of the fighting. No, he was only sad that a favorite cane had been broken in the tumult. The pianist said he would not punish him. Nevertheless, he took leave of the pianist and rushed outside into the darkness. He wandered for hours around the estate. At last, repentant, he decided to go back to the house and beg forgiveness of the servant. But despite a long search, he could not find the road, although from time to time the wind brought him the sound of the pianist improvising on an out of tune Bechstein.

This was the bad part of his story. The good part was this:

He came to a shed where a line of men waited. Inside the shed, he was told, was a beautiful woman who would marry the man with the gentlest touch. He decided to wait, too. At last, it was his turn. He entered the shed and saw a woman who was beautiful indeed. He touched her arm. "You are the gentlest," she said. "I shall marry you." And they were married that night, although he knew his touch was light not because he was gentle, but because he had wandered so many days without food that he was weak and nearly fainting from hunger.

Golden Moment

———

Arriving early for a dentist's appointment one morning, I go into Macy's, which is just across the street, and when I enter the men's department—the very moment I set foot among the shirts and ties— Pachelbel's Canon comes over the public-address system and the store is flooded with D Major—a key I associate with summer sunshine— and I beam serenely at men trying on slacks in front of multiple mirrors and at clerks lifting huge boxes of socks onto a counter with a sign proclaiming that, today, all Gold Toe socks are on sale with special low prices for ten pairs or more and, already, eager shoppers have amassed heaps of Gold Toe socks which, although essentially black, gray, and blue, do have gold stitching on their toes, and which, whatever their colors, are unquestionably bargains, I think, as I sweep down the aisle, as if across a flowered meadow in the Midi, while Pachelbel honeys the air with D Major and yellow-striped bumblebee-like sweaters blaze from display cases, and then I float out the door and ascend to the dentist high in a skyscraper where, as I sit in a chair with my mouth open in perpetual, but silent, exclamation, I realize I have just experienced a golden moment of epiphany.

II.
Perplexities

Research Topics

———

ablex
bannigans
chirmotherapy
delsterism
eglipsoids
the Fredonian heresy
gnittering
hachifrage
inner trilling
jarp
Kalongistan
legnum deposits
mollography
neo-delsterism
obscure wadings
patlotic hexameters
quiddling
regarpetude
Semajian scholarship
tixeprocity
usht
the varnish plebiscite
woadle
xurathenia
yaridian fits
zedaphobia

———

The Sincere Poet

The Sincere Poet is obsessed with the authenticity of his feelings. The Sincere Poet does not put a word to the page that he does not feel. For the Sincere Poet, every word he writes is a token of some true feeling he feels in his heart. The Sincere Poet's greatest enemies are false feelings. He thinks false feelings are counterfeit, like counterfeit coins: however brightly they shine, they are frauds nonetheless. What the Sincere Poet writes about is his suffering. He tells the Reader that he suffers and persuades the Reader that his sufferings are real.

Yet the Sincere Poet always wonders whether the Reader may be wondering whether the feelings in his poems are only fabrications: perhaps these are not genuine feelings, he fears the Reader may wonder, perhaps they are only feelings the Poet has made up. How can anyone be sure these feelings are real?

Therefore, the Sincere Poet must strive not only to feel, but to demonstrate the authenticity of his feelings. So he tears his feelings out of his flesh. He smears them in public on the page. He keeps on suffering ever more dreadful sufferings. His poetry raves, it jabbers, it shrieks. Yet the Sincere Poet cannot shake off two doubts: first, that the feelings he thinks are true are really false at heart; second, that no matter how true these feelings may be, they will always sound false to the Reader.

Thus, plagued with doubt, the Sincere Poet can never stop struggling to prove his sincerity. He must at all times demonstrate that he is genuine. At last, he writes a poem that says, "I will commit suicide." Then he commits suicide, that being one sure test of sincerity.

History teaches us that all Sincere Poets may be one day brought to this. It is only logical for Sincere Poets to commit suicide.

As a course of action, suicide is certainly effective. No wonder it is popular. Yet it is not the only effective course of action open to Sincere Poets. For example, a Sincere Poet could say in a poem, "I will now murder the Reader," and then do so—committing murder, like suicide, being a test of sincerity. Indeed, there is much to be said for this. With the Reader gone, the Sincere Poet no longer has to worry about whether or not anyone questions his sincerity. He can just write as he pleases. He doesn't even need to be sincere.

Bartenders

————

The best of them have names like Dave, Doug, Skeeter, Mitch, Kelly, Aldo, or Joe. They wear blue chambray or checked lumberjack shirts and tight jeans, are handsome in what you might call a rugged sensitive way. If it is easy to imagine them posing for physique photographs or cigarette ads, it is not wholly impossible to imagine them writing poetry or, at least, science fiction.

They stand behind their bars, fixing drinks. When business is slow they talk with the customers. They trade stories, they joke, they gossip a little, they listen to your troubles and try to give good advice. They also make sure no one gets too rowdy or drunk. Occasionally, they sip something from a glass, something colorless that fizzes. They say it's just club soda or tonic water, but you suspect there may be gin in that glass, or vodka. Everyone knows what they say about bartenders: that because they're near strong drink all the time, all bartenders, no matter how hard they resist, eventually become drunkards. First, it really is just tonic in that glass; then there's some gin mixed in to end the night, then a shot or two to start the evening right, and soon they're all drunks. That's why there's something melancholy about bartenders, no matter how hard they laugh. You're sure they are doomed.

That's what you think as you sit on your barstool. You're feeling good, it's nice and warm here. You decide you like that new bartender who serves you your drink. You could almost imagine him as a friend or a lover. But you can't. Not really.

That's the funny thing. Bartenders are mysterious. They have no existence outside their bars. You never see them anywhere else or know anyone who does. Once in a while, when you pass someone crossing the street, you think, "Gee, that looks like the bartender from the Sail Inn or the Roundup." But it's not. Oh no. Bartenders exist only in bars. Sometimes you hear rumors that this one has had several affairs or that one lived for years with a lover or gave parties that turned into wild orgies in his apartment. But such things are always in the past. At present, they're the guys behind the bar joking with the customers and getting the jukebox going when the place seems dead.

Though they're never really young—for you can tell they've been around—they're always young enough. They always look the same age: 29 or 39—some age you think is on the edge of changing soon (which is another reason why you find them melancholy). Yet their age never changes, never really. All that happens is that one day, without warning, you find they've been replaced. Skeeter is gone, and it's Mitch who is here now. Then Mitch gets replaced by this guy whose name you don't even know yet. ("It's Andy," he says.) And where do bartenders go when they move on from their bars? Sometimes to other bars. You see Skeeter again at the Roundup or the Sail Inn or the new place that's just opened around the corner. Yet he never looks quite like the Skeeter he used to be. You see bartenders at their best only in one bar.

But often you never see those bartenders again anywhere. They vanish away in the midst of the city. They disappear just like you do when you, too, leave the bar.

The Adventures of Bucky Badger

After all these years, I've got to tell this. I can't keep quiet any longer.

I was in Chicago, staying at a hotel. Two young-sounding guys had the room next to mine. That night, through the wall, I could hear them talking. And one guy told the other, "Whenever I came in, my college roommate used to say
　　say hi there Bucky Badger
Every time. He never failed. It gave him such a kick."

*

How cute. But what was that statement supposed to mean? And why did the roommate say it?

Perhaps it was a command. Perhaps the roommate was asking the guy
　　Say "Hi there, Bucky Badger"
—in which case, the guy would have to say
　　Hi there, Bucky Badger

Or perhaps *say* was not a command but a generalized exclamation akin to the British *I say!* or the American *hey!* In that case, the roommate was greeting the guy with a jolly
　　Say! Hi there, Bucky Badger

*

Who's Bucky Badger?

Presumably, neither the guy nor his roommate was a real badger. I also consider it unlikely, though just conceivable, that Bucky could have been either guy's first name and Badger his last. Yet *Bucky Badger* could easily have been the roommate's nickname for the guy. If so, that would support the theory that the remark was the roommate's madcap form of welcome.

However, other possibilities arise if the remark is interpreted as a command. Still assuming that *Bucky Badger* is the guy, the roommate

would then be ordering
  Say "Hi there," Bucky Badger
—to which the guy would have to reply
  Hi there

Yet *Bucky Badger* could also be the roommate's nickname for himself. In that case, the guy's response would have to be, as suggested in a previous speculation,
  Hi there, Bucky Badger

Then again, *Bucky Badger* may not actually refer to either of the guys. Perhaps the phrase was a tagline from some TV show I've never seen. Perhaps an authority on pop culture could instantly identify it and explain it to me. On the other hand, Wisconsin, which begins not very far north of Chicago, is nicknamed the Badger State, and Bucky Badger is the mascot of the University of Wisconsin. Perhaps the guy and his roommate went to Wisconsin and that statement was some kind of old campus slogan. But was that slogan
  Say hi there, Bucky Badger
or only
  Hi there, Bucky Badger?

*

Why does it matter? Why do I need to know? Why have I gone on wondering about this all these years? Why didn't I have the guts to bang on the wall and shout
  say! hi! there! Bucky! Badger!
and then wait to hear how that guy would respond? I might have settled the matter once and for all.

But I didn't do anything. I simply let them go on and change the subject. Next morning, they moved out. And here I am stranded with Bucky Badger.
  Say hi there
  Hi there
  Hi

The Pregnant Teapot

"Eek!" she screamed from the kitchen one morning. "Come in here and look! The teapot is pregnant."

"Nonsense!" I said. "How can a teapot be pregnant?"

"I don't know how, when, or why," she replied. "But just come in and look: this teapot is pregnant!"

Suddenly she accused me. "You did it!" she screamed. "You keep saying you want a cup of tea before bed. So you sit up all night. You sit up all night reading. You sit up all night thinking. I know you: you sit up all night dreaming of running away. And then you get horny and start humping the teapot."

There was nothing I could answer with her in that state. I just kept quiet, hoping she'd eventually calm down.

In any case, a few days later the teapot spawned a litter. Now there were little teacups all over the house.

They were hell to take care of. They had to be filled with tea. The tea had to be drunk. The cups had to be washed. And when they were washed they had to be dried. And soon it was time to fill them again.

Taking care of them wore me out, so I went to bed early. But she stayed up late, watching movies on television.

One day, blushing, she told me she was pregnant. There was a pregnant pause.

Finally, I whispered, "Who did it?" I looked around the room. I saw teapot, teacups, saucers, and spoons. I saw sugar bowl and creamer. I saw the TV set. There was another pregnant pause. Almost everything I looked at was pregnant now. And whatever wasn't pregnant was obviously horny.

Sunday Dinner

The year we became vegetarians, we fixed meat only for the cats. We'd set liver in the middle of the table and the cats would jump up and scrap over it. They would chase each other across the tabletop, spitting and snarling, knocking over the creamer and the salt shaker, and sometimes pulling the tablecloth and everything on it to the floor.

We decked ourselves out in our best superior looks and tried to sit as still as possible. The TV kept bringing back a documentary about the migration of lemmings. Cute and cuddly, bright and sassy, they frisked across a field on a sunny day. Decorous philosophical ghosts served us our food, which consisted primarily of boiled potatoes. We considered them inoffensive enough. Then one day, a potato got up in its plate and started to sing

> Five-feet-two, eyes of blue,
> But oh, what those five feet could do. . . .

Upon hearing this, we let the food drop from our gaping mouths and petrify on our plates. The cats posted themselves in lines along the walls and said, "We're waiting: try to explain this away, if you can. What fancy language are you going to use now? The vegetables are screaming for revenge." The cats suddenly jumped at us, clawing for our livers. While we fought them off, trying to convince them we suffered from cirrhosis, the potato thumped against its plate. The ghosts attended it with bated breath. On TV, the lemmings pattered down a slope in a cloud of dust and loose rocks, hurrying toward the sea. Some of the little buggers lost their footing in their excitement and toppled over the cliff, their heads bouncing off protruding boulders as they fell. By the time they hit the beach they were presumably dead. Undeterred, the rest of the lemmings scampered over the corpses and into the water.

Return to Work

I have returned to the job from which I was fired a whole decade ago. The funny thing is, no one recognizes me.

The same fat jolly bleached-blonde woman who was my department head then is my department head now. We get along well together. From the very first we share favorite jokes.

The same vice president who fired me then is vice president still. He is tall, skinny, nervous. He doesn't like my looks, he keeps lecturing me about duty. Yet he has to approve my appointment. What a bastard he is.

And there at their desks are all my pals from the old days: Bill, Carol, Russ, Al, Serena, David, Monty, and Cliff. Just as before.

And not one of them recognizes me. I have begun anew, totally anew.

Sometimes I think my fat blonde department head recognizes me. She smiles at me as though she's guessed my secret. But I know that's a subject she'll never bring up. Best of all, the skinny bastard vice president, though he may not like my looks, doesn't realize who I am.

So I sit at my desk as though I never sat there before. I sit there powerful in my secret knowledge. How wonderful.

I am a new man. How wonderful. How wonderful it is to return to work.

He Lives Among Us

———

Elvis lives:

he walks with us, he talks with us, he is always there, he has a farm in Wisconsin, a grocery in Seattle, he is a barfly in the Bronx, a bum who sleeps on cardboard over gratings, he's in the chorus at the Met, he's a sheriff in Missouri, a church organist in Duluth, a faith healer in Kentucky, he used to be a Baptist but now he's Jewish, he's a graduate student at Yale, an aide in the stacks at the Library of Congress, he works selling popcorn in the multiplex at the mall, he's shacking up with a floozie on the outskirts of Detroit, he's having an affair with James Dean on their Texas ranch, he goes around in drag, he's made himself into a Native American, renamed himself J. Turquoise Talltree, he's lost weight, gotten skinny, his hair's falling out, he's bald as an egg, he's grown a long beard, he stands in line on Tuesdays at your bank, he's in look-alike contests everywhere and never wins a one,

but seek him out, you'll find him, he's alive and well, is hidden yet among us, now and forevermore.

Amen.

My Mother Growing Old

Shortly after she had to move into the nursing home, she lost interest in seeing the snapshots of our trips—she who had loved to travel and was always eager to know where other people had been. Now she scarcely looked at the photos we brought her when we visited. Or she'd furrow her brow and ask, "Just what cathedral did you say this is? And where was that castle? I can't keep this stuff straight." And she'd brush the pictures aside. There soon came a time when she never even glanced at them.

But something started happening to the photos. I first noticed it in that one I took at the Grand Canyon. A shadowy figure stood by the guardrail I hadn't seen there before. It had been hazy at the canyon and nothing in that shot was very clear. Yet, after staring for a while, I had to admit, "You know, that could almost be Mother. She didn't go along with us that year, did she?" And, of course, she hadn't.

After that, she kept turning up in photos of other places I knew she'd never been. That woman on the Acropolis striding toward the Parthenon—that was surely Mother. And there was Mother beside an Alhambra fountain, Mother in a Venetian gondola, Mother at the Tower of London, and on the slopes of Mount Vesuvius. Mother had entered all our photographs.

Last summer in Paris, I unexpectedly saw her. One morning when we were strolling to Notre Dame, I saw Mother sipping coffee at a cafe table with a fine view of the cathedral. What shall I do? I wondered when I came near her. She certainly isn't expecting me. She doesn't look as if she needs anything. Yet how can I go by without speaking to her? So, though you held back, I went over and said, "Good morning. How nice to see you here. Fine day, isn't it?" She looked up, slightly surprised. But, after a moment, she smiled and replied, "Yes, indeed, such lovely weather we're having." Then, because neither of us could think of anything more to talk about and she still had her coffee and seemed happy to be there, I said good-bye and we parted.

Abandoned Cities

Asunción, Paraguay

Back of the adobe haciendas are reed huts set amongst the overseers' rotting privies. There, Indians wearing dirty loincloths are set to work with mortar and pestle to grind down strange metals: tungsten, bismuth, antimony, manganese. Although they are given a ration of a cup of brackish water every morning, the heat is so intense that their thirst remains unslaked. They are never allowed to leave their benches, not even to go to the toilet. As a result, streams of urine trickle constantly along the dirt floor, turning it to mud. The overseers are always drunk. Sometimes they waste whole afternoons by taking turns raping the Indian girls right there on the benches. But Indians and overseers alike are plagued by syphilitic fevers that rot the body with fits of shaking and green foam at the mouth. In front of the haciendas is Assumption Square, over which towers the Cathedral containing the remarkable Madonna of the Gourds, Bishop Laszlo's most precious treasure. At the opposite end of the square stands the Capitol. From time to time, the Secretary of the Interior stops counting his silver coins, looks out the window, grins, and spits tobacco juice onto the statue of Jesus Valdevinos-Feo at the Battle of Moltavis Rock which stands in the square below.

Bismarck, North Dakota

There are no suburbs. The streets stop at the wheat fields where the iron helmets are set on black sticks to frighten off eagles. Beyond this point, the wind begins, as hard to ignore as a stomachache. The townspeople fear two things always: drought and frost. Aldermen appear on television to blame infiltrators from the East. Revivalists set up tents in Courthouse Square, opposite the Granada Theatre where a movie is playing about the defeated tribes at the Battle of Moltavis

Rock. No one goes to the movies much these days. The balcony has been roped off since 1956. Some nights a strange wind hisses in from the prairies, covering the sidewalks with a thin layer of dust. Then everyone is frightened. A curfew is imposed. The sheriff searches the Yellow Pages for Negroes. But inside the houses Sunday dinners continue with gravy boats on the tables and fathers standing to say grace. Milking machines glitter in shop windows. Nevertheless, children flee daily to the wheat fields. Kids in baggy overalls crouch between the stalks and try to imitate the wind's hiss. Laszlo, the immigrant's son, is there, fingering the dress of a patient girl as they watch the state trooper's headlights vanish down Highway 27.

Kaunas, Lithuania

The walls and windowpanes are so clean people forget they are there. People forget things regularly, despite thick sweet cream in their coffee. On almost every parlor wall is a reproduction of Laszlo's famous painting, now in the National Gallery, of General Svedlin at the Battle of Moltavis Rock. It is the sky in that painting which is remarkable—one can even feel the breeze off the Baltic—so remarkable it becomes more real than the real sky above the real sea. The traffic comes and goes in great waves. Sometimes the streets—the widest boulevards as well as the lanes of the Old Town—are clogged with cars, bicycles, buses, and lorries barely able to inch forward. Then, suddenly, as though someone had forgotten about traffic, the streets are deserted. Even cripples and the most timid visiting goatherds from the farms can cross in mid-block without being run down. But where is there to go? The stores are empty now, as are the cafes, cups of coffee still steaming on the round white tables where minor bureaucrats sat only minutes before nibbling buns and discussing the news. As evidence of how much may be forgotten, one evening by the light of the signs in Market Square I asked the prostitutes who gather there what city they thought they were in. Many said Christiana, Danzig, Kovno, or Port Arthur. It was only after several hours of questioning that I found one who named a city I recognized, and I went home with her and paid her handsomely.

Ecbatana, Iran

There are two cities here, neither of which exists. By day, the site is a flat expanse of desert sand. But when a storm approaches, the wind makes the sand fly up into the air and momentarily assume the shapes of minarets, bazaars with squabbling merchants, the countinghouse of the Shah, camels on the highroad, and a great jeweled gate swinging open upon a sequestered private square with date palms and amaranths and veiled ladies eating sherbet beside a fountain whose clear water falls from the mouth of a stone lion into a mosaic basin with a sigh of tiny bells. At night, it is another city, a city built of shadows, whose sinister shapes loom imposingly, then melt as one draws near. Yet one may catch glimpses of leprous beggars in rags, of English schoolmasters buggering little boys, and of the explorer Laszlo near the end of his life trying to find solace in a haze of kef. Then the voice of the Prophet thunders across the desert, "Abandon the desolate places and the places of deceit. Set yourself upon the path of wisdom and take heed that, unlike the mighty chieftain Ahmid Faz, you are not felled by an assassin's arrow watching wild horses race in the moonlight across the plain toward the Sea of Marmora while on your way home victorious from the Battle of Moltavis Rock."

Superfluous

No, you shall not be hurt. You may depart at once. All that is required is that you wear this placard reading, I am an ugly thing because I am superfluous. You may go where you like. You may even come back and visit or dine with me in public. Only you must at all times wear the placard reading, I am an ugly thing because I am superfluous. You must never take it off. At home, in the street, awake, asleep—you must wear the placard. Should you by any chance be foolish enough to feel humiliated and so commit suicide because of this, it will make no difference. I shall conceal the news of your death and have someone else dressed like you go about wearing the placard reading, I am an ugly thing because I am superfluous. Everyone will still think it is you. For with that placard, it could only be you. That is why the placard is necessary, and why you, except as its wearer, are superfluous.

The Model Community

The Superintendent was showing me through the Model Community. "It is finished at last," he beamed, "and it has worked out splendidly, just as planned.

"Of course," he conceded, "there are still a few hitches, some slight imperfections. But, I assure you, we are doing our best to correct them."

However, as I looked about, it seemed to me as if the imperfections were serious indeed. Take shopping. There were many stores scattered throughout the town, but it was impossible to tell what they had in stock on any given day. One store might have butter. But bread would have to be bought at another store far off on the east side. Or a store might have meat. But the only potatoes would be in a store on the west side. And no one knew what stores would have what goods tomorrow. Shoppers had to dash from store to store and, since all the stores had long lines in front of them, tempers soon frayed.

Everything in the Model Community may have been part of a plan, yet it was often impossible to discern the plan's rationale. Thus the hospital—one place where quiet was surely essential—looked out upon a truck route and was next door to a foundry.

The bicycle path was a narrow strip in the middle of an automobile expressway and, in just the few minutes that I stood watching traffic, there were several near-collisions between motorists and cyclists. Children going to the municipal playground had to cross that same highway—and at their own risk, for no one had thought to put in an overpass, an underpass, or even a stoplight. The grinding of brakes and honking of horns never ceased. And, every few minutes, a siren wailed.

Next, the Superintendent led me through some model apartments. Many were attractive, yet each had something wrong with it. One had a sink, but no toilet. Another had a toilet, but no sink, whereas the toilet in the third one was for some reason in the living room.

Nevertheless, the Superintendent kept beaming, "Isn't this splendid? And all according to plan."

Finally, unable to restrain myself, I said, "But, surely, more work needs to be done. Surely mistakes have been made. Why, the apartment we're in now has neither closets nor windows."

The Superintendent was horrified. "But that," he protested, "was part of the plan. It is all as planned. This is the Model Community.

"In this community," he explained, "every aspect of work and play is so arranged as to demand one's undivided attention. You can't breeze through the day here. You must concentrate on even your slightest task or pastime—which is all to the good, for the unexamined life is not worth living.

"Of course," he admitted, "there are still a few hitches, some slight imperfections. But we are doing our best to correct them. Ah, yes!" And, bending over, he snipped the telephone cord.

Your Last Phone Call

———

They do nothing to trouble you. It's really very nice here. But they'd rather have you out. In fact, they'd rather have you dead. Just to make things tidier.

That's why they've installed this other telephone, the one with the notice that says, "Warning: This apparatus is fatal. Lift the receiver and the doors and windows will automatically lock and poison gas will seep from the mouthpiece. Therefore use this phone only when necessary."

There it sits, right next to the regular phone, the one that connects you to the outside world. Give them credit: they've labeled it, they're fair. Yet the thing remains bothersome.

Someone could pick it up by accident, perhaps stumbling confused in the middle of the night or so engrossed in thought as to forget which phone is which. Then, too, the thing casts a spell. It's always there. Its presence gets to you. It makes you wonder, does it really work? You stare at it in horror, and then in fascination until at last—you don't know why—you pick it up. But now it's too late. You've placed your call. The line is busy with your death.

There are also those who use it because they choose to. They want to order their own deaths the way they'd phone to order take-out pizza. Of course, if they were tired of it here, they could simply leave. It can be done. But where would they go? And how would they manage there? So, they decide, better end it, get it over with, once and for all.

That's the sort of person it's hoped you'll be. That's why, after a while here, it's expected you'll make your call. They don't mind you here, of course. It's a very nice place. But they'd rather have you gone. If possible, for good.

———

Phalaris and the Bull:
A Story and an Examination

The Story:

The tyrant Phalaris locked his prisoners inside a magnificently wrought brazen bull and tortured them over a slow fire. So that nothing unseemly might spoil his feasting, he commanded the royal artisans to design the bull in such a way that its smoke rose in spicy clouds of incense. When the screams of the dying reached the tyrant's ears, they had the sound of sweet music. And when the bull was reopened, the victims' bones shone like jewels and were made into bracelets.

The Examination:

1. This story appears to be allegorical. Of what is it an allegory?

2. Which person or persons do you consider most vile: the tyrant Phalaris, the artisans who carried out his orders, or the court ladies who wore the bone bracelets?

3. Do you think it right that your sympathy extends almost automatically to the victims? But do you know who the victims were or why they were condemned? What if the victims had been Hitler and your twelve least favorite contemporary political figures—would this knowledge affect your sympathies?

4. Do you not sometimes wish that certain people might die, do you not long for the deaths of prime ministers or dictators, do you not envision presidents dying of heart attacks, generals shooting themselves while cleaning their rifles, skinflint landlords pushed into wells by rebellious peasants, industrialists skidding on newly waxed floors and sailing through penthouse windows, War Department scientists exposed to radiation while goosing cute researchers in the lab, demagogues exploding with the leaky gas main, your mother-in-law

scalded by a pot of boiling chicken soup—do you not wish any or all of these were dead?

5. If the death of one man could bring bliss to the world, would you order that one death? If the deaths of two men could do it, would you order those two deaths? Or five deaths? Or a hundred? Or twenty million? How many deaths would you order to bring bliss to the world?

6. If it required only one man's death, after all, to bring bliss to the world and you sanctioned such a death, how would you feel should you learn that that one man was to be you?

7. Do you think that the most monstrous thing about the story of Phalaris is not that a tyrant put prisoners to death—since that has happened throughout history—but the particularly gruesome way he went about it?

8. Yet do you never catch yourself wishing that once, only once, once only but definitely once, you could sit beside the tyrant just to satisfy your curiosity about what the bull looked like, what the music sounded like?

9. Would you consider Phalaris and his artisans more, or less, reprehensible if the screams of the dying had reached the ear undisguised? If you were one of the victims, would it make any difference to you?

10. Which do you consider the more truly good man: the victim who wishes his screams to be heard as screams, or he who wishes them to be heard as music? Do you think your answer is relevant to the problem of why at executions we praise the victim who meets his death with stoic calm and witty epigrams, rather than he who must be dragged to the scaffold pissing in his pants? In your opinion, is it or is it not a good thing that we do so?

11. Learning at this point in the examination that the first victim of the bull was the chief artisan who designed it, do you (a) believe that the artisan deserved his fate?, and (b) feel vaguely uncomfortable about your own occupation, job, profession, or calling? Why or why not?

12. Based on your interpretation of the story of Phalaris and the bull, do you view yourself in the light of your present situation in life as metaphorically equivalent to tyrant, artisan, victim, or wearer of bone jewelry?

13. And which am I?

The White Chapter

———

In this part of the story you wake up and find that everything is white. Morning and evening alike, the sky will be washed by searchlights. Stout women in aprons will glide past both sides of your bed carrying plates of dumplings. The knives will be sheathed in wool, the ice pick embedded in cotton. When you cry, your tears will spread like cream around oatmeal. Nothing will be stained, nothing spotted. With your toes in plaster, like capped teeth, you will cross streets of crude rubber. So you do not skid into unmarked pits, the miners will scatter salt in your path. Nothing you meet with will be harsh. Strangers will hand their words to you wrapped in flour, and you will sift them grain by grain until the vowels lose their accents. You will discover the secret of stones, that stones are really made of hair coiled tightly upon itself. And you will learn how to unfasten the hair of stones until a stone flows soft as linen. From then on, nothing will pass away. You will stare at your pale swollen belly as though it were the moon. The suicides leaping from the windows of office buildings will hang in the air like suspended loaves of bread. The farm boy brought before the firing squad will have the white handkerchief painted indelibly upon his eyes.

———

Snow

Fine white bread is sold in Helsingfors in a little kiosk beside the permanent snow.

Snow is a great enigma. If you tear off a handful, it looks exactly the same inside and out. We are not like that. Tear off our clothes and there is skin that is not the same as clothes. Tear off the skin and we are dead, all of us, quite dead.

Twice an hour people leave the tram cars and stand in line for the fine white bread. They talk of apple butter and the deaf-mutes draw happy pictures of it. Like snow, bread is a great enigma. The waiting people cannot understand bread because it is bread all the way through. But they know that bread is good, is not to be found everywhere, and is never to be found in a snowbank.

They do not like snow even though it is something like bread. There is too much snow in this world, they think. They throw stones at the snow and stoves fat as archbishops. But the snow keeps coming back from the sky. The bread goes. It does not come back. Three slow grandmothers must go home without bread. The snow remains where it always was. It looks like bread without a crust. It is not good to eat. In the Lesser Antilles it is worshipped as a god.

Moral Discourse

There were these three prisoners. All three had heads on their shoulders. The fact that they were prisoners didn't mean they were stupid. Indeed, they had a serious talk. At least, two of them did. The third mostly kept his mouth shut while the others spoke about him. He was widely held to be innocent, the victim of injustice and, what's more, was said to be some sort of wise man.

That riled the first one, who grumbled, "If you're so smart, why didn't you do something to get us out of this?"

But the second one interrupted, "Well, we did do what they say we did. Let's face it: we deserve this, we really can't complain. So why whine? But this guy's different. He ought to complain. Yet he's taking it like a man."

This conversation went on while all three were dying on crosses. They pondered what might have been and what could be; they mulled over innocence, guilt, and responsibility while nails were tearing into their flesh.

At least, that's what Luke says. But Luke, or whoever wrote those words, never says anything about pain. Surely, there must have been pain, excruciating pain. Yet Luke overlooks it. Instead, he focuses upon moral issues, philosophical problems, sober (if occasionally grumpy) discourse. This is how he views the scene. Others might see it otherwise.

For instance, when Jesus tells the second prisoner, "Today shalt thou be with me in paradise," someone might wonder why he didn't make that same promise to the first guy who did, after all, raise a genuinely provocative issue and hadn't bothered with flattery. But another observer might be conscious only of the pain. And someone else might ask, "In such a situation, what's the point of discussing anything?"

True or False Quiz

———

1. A yellow cat is sitting in my doorway. (T___ F___)
2. There are mysterious footsteps in the hall. (T___ F___)
3. They are planning to murder my sister. (T___ F___)
4. I am hungry. (T___ F___)
5. My breath smells either of garlic or of toothpaste. (T___ F___)
6. I had a letter published pseudonymously in yesterday's *Times*. (T___ F___)
7. I shall have sex tomorrow. (T___ F___)
8. Someone is sending me money. (T___ F___)
9. Someone is thinking of someone else with my name. (T___ F___)
10. All this is really an attempt to describe a mystical experience. (T___ F___)
11. Boys were playing ball in the street when I wrote this. (T___ F___)
12. On my dresser are three coins and a ticket stub. (T___ F___)
13. The light over my sink has burned out. (T___ F___)
14. There is another questionnaire like this on my desk. (T___ F___)
15. I have started smoking again on the sly. (T___ F___)
16. I am not wearing any underwear. (T___ F___)
17. I love you. (T___ F___)
18. I am telling a lie. (T___ F___)
19. When I go into the bedroom something surely will happen. (T___ F___)
20. If I had walked with you last night we would have seen the stars. (T___ F___)

———

III.

Journeys

A Journey by Railroad

I was on an express with no stops scheduled. Yet the train slowed as it approached a platform, then braked to a halt. No one knew why.

At last, a voice came over the public-address system: "This is the conductor speaking. The engineer has decided to stop here because this town has one of his favorite restaurants. He invites you to follow him for a real taste treat."

Laughing nervously, we spilled onto the platform and straggled up Main Street. Well, I had to admit, I do like a nice meal. Still, this is a pretty odd way to get to know a restaurant.

I also had to admit that the town wasn't much. In fact, it looked dumpy. We passed block after block of ramshackle houses with sagging porches and at last reached the restaurant. "Here we are, folks," the engineer shouted.

I can't say I felt heartened. The joint seemed hardly more than a saloon. Yet good meals can sometimes be had in unexpected places.

A shuffling waitress slapped down a gravy-stained menu. "Well," she said, "what'll it be?" Most of the items had already been scratched out, yet I managed to order. It took a long time for anything to arrive and, then, all the hot dishes were cold. But after looking around at my fellow passengers, I decided they were no better off than I was. Several were complaining about dirty forks. One had found a bug in the soup.

The engineer was sitting at the bar. Even though he was the one guy who claimed he liked the food here, he was eating very little. But he was drinking quite a lot, and the way he teetered on his barstool made me suspect he was plastered, a suspicion confirmed when he fell unconscious to the floor, whereupon the bartender and the cook carried him off into the kitchen. And that was the last we saw of him.

What, we wondered, would happen now? The conductor got up, cleared his throat, and said, "I'm afraid we're stuck. The engineer, as you see, is indisposed. And because our train is still on the track, no other trains can pass through. So until our engineer regains his health and can move the train, I suggest we find accommodations at some hotel."

"Ain't no hotels here," the waitress interjected. "No motels, neither."

"Then what I'd suggest," the conductor sighed, "is to go through the streets knocking on doors in search of hospitality." We did. But either no one responded or the doors were slammed when our needs were made known. And when I heard what sounded like a shotgun going off, I beat a hasty retreat.

We gathered, crestfallen, back at the restaurant. "Is there anyone here who knows how to drive a train?" the conductor asked in desperation. Of course, no one did.

Suddenly, he turned to me. "What about you? You look pretty smart." I blushed to hear it. "I bet you've even been to college." Which I couldn't deny. "So come on, drive this train for us." And before I could protest, he was dragging me back to the depot.

When we reached the engine he rummaged around and pulled out an engineer's cap, a blue chambray work shirt, and a pair of bib overalls. "Try them," he said. "It can get pretty greasy in there." I put them on. To my surprise, they fit rather well. I even fancied I cut a good figure in them. Maybe it won't be so bad, after all. It's actually nice and cozy here in the cab. And is there anyone who didn't want to drive a train as a kid?

Then the conductor—as good a soul as ever I've met—showed me where the whistle was. What a brave sound it makes. Listen! How lovely. And look: how the tracks shine up ahead!

Let's go.

Life on the Moon

———

Like anyplace else, it has its problems. It also has its advantages, especially when it's waxing. Then we step forth from our huddle, happy to find one more inch of ground to hold us. And the ground continues to spread on all sides until it stretches as far as we can see. Men and women stride this way and that and never bump into anyone. Children gambol on the leas. Rabbits bound across the moors. Sometimes we dance for hours on end—that is, until someone feels the ground slip out from under his feet and someone else hears a faint rustle of pebbles that gradually becomes a rattle of stones. We know this can mean only one thing: the waning has begun. It continues. The ground shrinks. It trembles. Canyons open, gorges yawn, avalanches bear whole cliffs away. One must be careful where one steps, for where the ground does not crumble it turns ominously spongy. In time, one grows adept at hopping from stone to stone for safety. But newcomers here—and even some of our very own elderly—often prove not quite quick enough. So they vanish forever into outer space. At last, there is almost no ground left. We're joined together in a huddle once more and, still, some people can't find a toehold. They, too, float off from us. At last comes the moment even old-timers dread: the moment we feel nothing at all beneath our feet. It's only for an instant, yet it's real. Now nothing exists but terror and the void, for no matter how often we've lived through this, we still fear we are doomed. Yet we also try to summon up faith and reason out that all is not lost. And we are right: a sliver of ground firms to support our feet—only a sliver, yet it is there. We are saved again, safe on the solid ground of a newborn moon.

A Reading of This Poem

It is evident from the very first words that the subject of the poem under consideration is a late summer afternoon in New York City.

You will observe that, following a generalized setting of the scene, the poet continues with a reference to gay people strolling through the streets of Greenwich Village. It soon becomes apparent that he is not using "gay" solely in the sense of meaning "bright" or "lively" (although these meanings are not entirely irrelevant, for part of the point of the poem is the amiability of the occasion being described); nevertheless, even taking into account these implications, it should be obvious that the poet is using "gay" primarily as a synonym for "homosexual"—and, in this specific instance, "homosexual male." Next, the poet calls attention to certain aspects of the aforementioned people: their casual manner, their laughter, their tanned skin, their open shirts revealing hints of hairy or hairless chests, the tightness of their jeans and possible lack of underwear, and, most importantly, their ease and self-confidence. The poet speculates upon whether this is due merely to the time of year and current men's fashions, or whether these qualities result from the new militant gay activism. In any case, the poet praises the friendly way in which we are greeted.

Notice here how the poet has slyly introduced the first person plural into his poem, assuming that we would not find it embarrassing to be amongst these people. Look, the poet says, one of them is putting his arm around you as he talks. And what is he talking about? The poet offers no details, but we can imagine such topics as films and records, perhaps, or ballet, travel, politics, or poetry. The poet does intimate, though, that the conversation is charming and intelligent. It certainly cannot be objectionable to you, for the poet deliberately takes several lines to emphasize that much time has elapsed since the start of all this, and you are still listening, apparently still interested. Then a drink is suggested: "Why don't you come up to my place for a drink?"

Take note: our terms are "you" and "I" now. The poet is propositioning you. So how about it? If you are bright, lively, and gay, why not say "yes" to me?

The Party Train

To bring joy and friendliness to the New York subway system, which is all too often bleak and indifferent, I propose that a special train be instituted to be known as The Party Train. Each day, this train would follow one or another of the city's existing routes, sometimes on the local, sometimes on the express tracks. No extra fare would be charged, the cars would be painted exactly the same as those of any other train, but inside there would be a perpetual party. The poles and straps would be festooned with streamers, and Japanese lanterns would hang from the ceiling. Food and drink would always be available, ranging from corned beef to caviar, from beer to champagne. Strolling musicians would roam from car to car. And the last car would be transformed into a gigantic bed where anyone could take a date, no questions asked.

The Party Train would not only be fun to ride, the very knowledge of its existence would be a source of cheer. For the route it would follow on any given day would never be announced in advance, but would always come as a fresh surprise. Thus any citizen waiting in any station could hope that the next train to pull in—accompanied by a shower of confetti and a whiff of pot smoke—would be The Party Train, so he could step aboard and glut himself on cashew nuts and kisses from the Battery to the Bronx. Or if he were in a local station and The Party Train happened to be an express that day, he could watch it rumble by, glimpsing paper hats and saxophones bouncing in the front cars and naked bodies flickering among the pillows at the back. Then he would chuckle to himself, glad that there was something interesting to look at while waiting for the subway, and wishing that tomorrow The Party Train might finally stop for him.

A Window in the Poem

———

In painting after painting—sacred or secular—of the fifteenth and sixteenth centuries, there is a window. What it looks out upon may have nothing to do with the painting's ostensible subject. Yet, perhaps, for that very reason it does.

Consider, dear reader. I open this window. Behold:

The infant Jesus rests in Mary's lap. Behind them, through a window, you can see a clearing where monks are building a monastery several centuries later. All this is easy to explain.

So let us pass on. Here is a man—a merchant? a lawyer?—who's intent upon reading a document black with cobwebs of words. He squints at it, puzzles over it. His face is wrinkled. Yet, surely, he is not as old as he appears. And if he would only turn his head and gaze out the window, he could see a river gliding between forested banks. Look out that window now. How prosperous, how peaceful, things seem there. Wouldn't it be nice to hire a boat and float down that stream?

There is a window in these paintings to remind us that there is always something else: whatever happens, something else is also going on, or something else can be found in time by following this river or by venturing into that clearing.

Take, for example, this road you'll see in just a few seconds. Right now, though, Jesus has paused, looking patient and very vulnerable, to let Thomas place his fingers on his wounds. Look there: Thomas is touching him. And, see, there is an arched window behind them. And see through the window how an empty road winds uphill among trees. The road looks steep, dusty. But all the leaves on the trees are fresh and green. Where do you suppose the road is going? Would you travel it if you could? Would you risk it? Would you dare?

But in this painting the bound man has no chance of ever reaching the city whose banners can be glimpsed through the window at his back. He stares out in your direction. And you, too, have to stare. If you ran off now toward the city, would this be bravery or cowardice?

Angels

Essentially, they are alike. And no one has ever seen one, for there is nothing there to see.

Those who think they see them see only their trappings: their garments, perhaps, or their passing expressions, but never their actual features: they have none. Yet they do exist, they are real.

Still, all we know of them is through appearances, the likenesses they don to bring their messages to us. They come here solely to deliver their messages. That is the reason for their being. They are their messages. And those messages are urgent, always.

That is why they put on guises, why they work their way into our consciousness. That is why they come as someone strange but interesting, someone who attracts your attention, someone tugging at your sleeve, someone with flashing eyes, someone making you wonder so much you are caught in a spell and you attend to the message.

Now only the message remains, while its bearer, however intriguing or alluring, disappears. You find yourself alone, totally alone, bearing the weight of these tidings: inexplicable, overwhelming, unbelievable, to be believed.

Traffic

———

There is the traffic. Outside the window. At all hours. It comes and goes. Surges. Recedes. Like thoughts. Like breath. Anyone's breath. Anonymous. Yet particular. You can hear it. Even with your back turned. There it is. The traffic. Coming and going. At any hour. Any time of day. Yet always coming out of night. Always going into night. Into darkness. Beyond our hearing. Out of sight. But at this point there is traffic. It is there. Like a thought. Like breathing. Like the breath of anyone. Of anyone out there in those cars. Anonymous. Particular. There. Like our breathing. First in. Then out.

About the Author

Jack Anderson, a poet and dance writer, is the author of eight previous books of poetry and seven books of dance history and criticism. His volumes of poetry include *Field Trips on the Rapid Transit* (Hanging Loose Press), *The Clouds of That Country* (Hanging Loose Press), *The Invention of New Jersey* (University of Pittsburgh Press), and *Selected Poems* (Release Press). His poems have appeared in many literary magazines and in various anthologies, among them *American Poets Say Goodbye to the Twentieth Century*, ed. by Andrei Codrescu and Laura Rosenthal; *Queer Dog*, ed. by Gerry Gomez Pearlberg; *Vital Signs: Contemporary American Poetry from the University Presses*, ed. by Ronald Wallace; *Epiphanies: The Prose Poem Now*, ed. by George Myers, Jr.; and *The Prose Poem: An International Anthology*, ed. by Michael Benedikt. Anderson has been writing prose poems since the 1960s and one of his prose poems provided the title for the New Rivers Press anthology *The Party Train* (1996).

He has read his poems at colleges and cultural centers in the United States, Canada, England, and Australia. He has been a visiting writer at the College of DuPage (Illinois) and poet-in-residence at the University of Kansas, and has received both a National Endowment for the Arts creative writing fellowship and a National Endowment literary award.

Anderson is a dance critic for the *New York Times*, New York correspondent for *The Dancing Times* of London, and coeditor (with George Dorris) of *Dance Chronicle*, a journal of dance history. His most recent dance book is *Art Without Boundaries: The World of Modern Dance* (University of Iowa Press), an international history of modern dance. He has taught dance history and criticism at the University of Adelaide (Australia), the North Carolina School of the Arts, the University of Minnesota, the College of St. Catherine (St. Paul, Minnesota), the New School for Social Research, Herbert L. Lehman College (New York City), and the American Dance Festival.

He has been a member of the National Endowment for the Arts Dance Panel and the deputy dance critic of the *Daily Mail* (London). He received the José de la Torre Bueno Award for dance writing for his book, *The One and Only: The Ballet Russe de Monte Carlo.*